Let Us Go Over to Bethlehem

JAMES W. MOORE

Let Us
Go Over to
Bethlehem

AN ADVENT STUDY FOR ADULTS

ABINGDON PRESS / Nashville

LET US GO OVER TO BETHLEHEM:
AN ADVENT STUDY FOR ADULTS

Copyright © 2001 by Abingdon Press

This book is printed on acid-free paper.

ISBN 0-687-09809-2

01 02 03 04 05 06 07 08 09 10—10 9 8 7 6 5 4 3 2 1
MANUFACTURED IN THE UNITED STATES OF AMERICA

In honor of

the great and gracious members and staff

of

St. Luke's United Methodist Church,

Houston, Texas

Contents

Introduction

"Frequent-flyer Syndrome"

I had a fascinating, thought-provoking experience on an airplane recently. I was seated beside a woman who had never flown before. She was absolutely delightful! She was like a little child—so thrilled, so excited, and so exhilarated to be on an airplane for the very first time. She was the epitome of wide-eyed wonder.

"I've never flown before," she said to me. "I'm sixty-two years old, and this is my first time on an airplane. Isn't this wonderful? It's so exciting, so thrilling! Just think, this huge, heavy plane with all these people and all this cargo will actually fly through the sky. It's amazing! It's incredible! It's a miracle!

It was fun for me to watch her. She was seizing and celebrating the moment, relishing this new, exciting experience. She was into it. She was focused. She was taking it all in.

She tested her seat belt several times. She checked and rechecked the reading lamp above her. She adjusted the air vent repeatedly. She located all the emergency exits and pointed them out to me. She patted my hand and informed me with a whisper that if the flight attendant offered me a soft drink, it would be OK to take it because it was already paid for in the ticket price. She found the safety procedure instruction card in the pouch on the back of the seat in front of her, and she read it out loud to me—twice! She gave me a play-by-play description of the loading of the luggage, and she became especially animated when she saw her luggage glide up the ramp and into the plane. When the flight attendants stood in the aisle of the plane and gave their instructions, she took notes!

It was a wonderful, electric, magical moment for her, a moment she had dreamed about all her life. Now it was happening for her, and she was thrilled beyond belief.

As I sat beside this woman and experienced air travel through her fresh and appreciative eyes, I was touched; and I was sensitized to all that was going on around us and how truly amazing it all really was. I just got a big kick out of watching her savoring the experience and basking in the glow of that moment.

But then I looked around. What do you think the other people on the plane were doing? That's right; they were

sleeping
thumbing through magazines
writing letters
reading novels
listening to tapes
perusing newspapers
working with lap-top computers
playing hand-held electronic games.

And most of the other passengers looked either bored or preoccupied. You know why, don't you? They were "frequent flyers"! They had been down this road before. They had flown this flight before. They had made this trip before. They had experienced air travel before, so there was nothing new or fresh or exciting or invigorating about it.

No magic! No wonder! No miracle! No inspiration! No appreciation! No exhilaration! No excitement! It was old hat, routine, the same old grind, business as usual, just going through the motions again because most of the people on the plane that day (myself included) had become "victims" of what we might call "Frequent-flyer Syndrome."

As I thought about that, I suddenly realized something; and it hit me like a bolt out of the blue: This Frequent-flyer Syndrome is the problem, the challenge, the temptation that we face as we make our spiritual journey through life. Sadly,

we often miss the joy of the moment;
we often lose the excitement of the experience;
we sometimes fail to feel the presence of God;
we sometimes take for granted what
    God has done for us in Jesus Christ;
and we sometimes miss the miracles
    of God's grace that are all around us

because we have become "frequent flyers"—tuned-out, preoc-cupied, bored, unmoved, uninspired—just stonewalling our way through life. "I've been down this road before; pass me a magazine." "I've flown this flight before; think I'll take a nap." This Frequent-flyer Syndrome is dangerous. It is a spiritual poison that can devastate our souls. It can desensitize us and dampen our spirits. It can rob us of the vitality and joy of life and lull us into a spiritual lethargy. It can cut us off from our Lord. Let me show you what I mean.

First of All, We Can Have Frequent-flyer Syndrome With Christmas

Most of us "grownups" have made this trip to Bethlehem so many times before. Sometimes we become travel-weary and preoccupied; and we stonewall through it all, saying, "If we can just make it through December..."

But not so with the children. They are excited and exhila-rated by the miracle of Christmas! They are not jaded or cal-lused or cynical. They approach the manger with wide-eyed wonder.

A mother and father went Christmas shopping one Saturday afternoon with their seven-year-old daughter. The little girl was so thrilled about Christmas, so happy, so enthusiastic, so alive to the season. But her parents were just the opposite, so grumpy, so grouchy, so tense, so uptight, so worn out with traf-fic jams and lists and bills and long lines.

When the family returned home that night, the little girl was singing Christmas carols; but her mother and father were cross, snapping at each other. Finally, the father, in an agitated tone, told the little girl to stop that singing and go to bed.

The little girl started upstairs to her room; but she stopped on the stairway, opened the window, and looked out. "Why did you open the window and let in the cold air?" her father asked. "Because I thought I heard the angels singing," she answered. Still angry and tired, the father said, "I don't hear any angels singing, and neither do *you*. Now get on upstairs, and get in that bed right now!" The little girl started up the stairs; but then she paused and said gently, "Daddy, if you want to hear the angels sing, you have to listen with your heart." Then she kindly hugged her father and moved on upstairs to her bed.

Maybe that is the sort of thing Jesus had in mind when he said, "Truly I tell you, whoever does not receive the kingdom of God as a little child will never enter it" (Mark 10:15). Maybe that is why God chose John the Baptist to prepare the way for the Messiah and to shake the world out of its doldrums. John, with his shaggy hair, leather girdle, and camel's hair robe, eating locusts and wild honey and shouting in the wilderness, must have been a sight to behold! This was high drama with a purpose.

God knew about the Frequent-flyer Syndrome, and God also knew that the world needed a powerful "wake-up call" to get our attention and to show us that the Savior had come into the world.

That is the number one danger of Frequent-flyer Syndrome: We can have Frequent-flyer Syndrome with Christmas.

Second, We Can Have Frequent-flyer Syndrome With Our Loved Ones

Robert Rodale (1930–1990) built a $250 million company as an environmentalist. In 1990, at the age of sixty (a *youthful* sixty), Rodale was suddenly and tragically killed in a car wreck. Mike McGrath, Rodale's coworker and close friend at Rodale Press, tells of his horror when he learned of the death of his friend:

What I learned—and learned hard—is that you can never really be *sure* that you'll ever see someone again. So it's best to not leave business undone; feelings unspoken. Bob's passing has taught me that when we say goodbye to someone, it may well be the last time we see that person. It *probably* won't be; but it *could* be.

Anyone who walks out a door just might be walking out of your life forever. So pay a compliment. Say something nice you've been meaning to say to someone. Tell them that you think they're a good, talented person; that you value their friendship; that you admire their ability; that they make you happy . . .

It's a notion that you'll never regret.[1]

Listen! It is so important, so crucial. Do not go to sleep at the switch with your loved ones. In other words, do not take them for granted. Let them know how much you appreciate them. If you need to say "I love you" or "Thank you" or "I'm sorry" to someone, what are you *waiting* for? *Say* it! Do not put it off any longer! Do not be preoccupied, travel-weary "frequent flyers" with your loved ones. Celebrate and express the miracle of love!

Those are the first two dangers: We can be "frequent flyers" with Christmas, and we can be "frequent flyers" with our loved ones.

Third and Finally, We Can Have Frequent-flyer Syndrome With God

Dr. Eddie Fox, the Director of World Evangelism for the World Methodist Council, was here in our church recently. At a luncheon in our parlor, he and some of his coworkers were telling us about some of the amazing things that are happening now in the former Soviet Union.

The people there who were under Communist rule for so many years are now free to worship God as they choose, and new churches are springing up all over the place. Dr. Fox and members of his group described how thrilling it is to see these people hungrily coming to God and how excited and exhilarated and beautifully childlike they are in their faith and commitment.

One of the members of Dr. Fox's group at that luncheon was a minister from Estonia named Olav Parnamets. When Olav came forward to speak, the master of ceremonies said, "Before

Olav speaks, I want to lead us in prayer." He then proceeded to place his hand on Olav's shoulder and to pray a simple prayer: He thanked God for Olav and his ministry and for the great things happening now in the churches in Estonia, and then he thanked God for sending Jesus Christ into the world to be our Savior.

When the prayer was concluded, I opened my eyes; and I was touched and inspired by what I saw. I was seated at the front table, and Olav was standing right in front of me. I was so close that I could have reached out and touched him. When I looked up into his face, here is what I saw: Big tears of joy were streaming down Olav's cheeks; and God was there.

For most of us "frequent flyers" in that room, this had been a routine prayer. But not for Olav! Olav was moved to tears by the very thought of Jesus Christ. The very thought of Jesus Christ coming into the world to save us moved Olav to tears of joy and gratitude.

Let me ask you something: How long has it been since you were moved like that? How long has it been since you had a spiritual experience that touched you so powerfully, so profoundly, that you were moved to tears of joy and appreciation for what God has done for us in Jesus Christ?

Don't be a "frequent flyer" with Christmas this year.

Don't be a "frequent flyer" with your loved ones.

Don't be a "frequent flyer" with God.

Seize the moments! Celebrate the miracles! Feel the joy! If you listen with your heart, you can hear the angels sing. If you open your heart, the Christ Child will come in.

NOTE

[1] From "In Memorium," by Mike McGrath, in *Save Three Lives*, by Robert Rodale (San Francisco: Sierra Club Books, 1992); pages XVI–XVII. See *Homiletics*, October-December, 1992.

Let Us Go Over to Bethlehem and Find the Faith of Christmas

Scripture: Read Luke 2:15-20.

Recently, I ran across a fascinating list called "Ten Commandments for Christmas." I would like to share these with you as we move into the season of Advent. I found them helpful to think about as we begin our journey toward Christmas, and I hope that you will too. Here they are:

Ten Commandments for Christmas:

1 *Thou shalt prepare early.* Don't wait until the last minute to get into the Christmas spirit.
2 *Thou shalt keep Christ at the center of Christmas.* Don't allow yourself to be overwhelmed by the commercialism of the season. Resolve to read one of the Gospels during December, and meditate upon what it means that Christ came into the world.
3 *Thou shalt make Christmas a family time.* Do things together: Decorate the tree, play games, bake cookies, shop, write cards, have devotionals, go caroling, attend church together.
4 *Thou shalt remember those who are less fortunate.* Contribute significantly to an organization serving the needs of others throughout the year. Give a Christmas gift to your church.
5 *Thou shalt give thyself with every gift.* Put some thought into the gifts you purchase. Give a gift that represents you. If possible, make something instead of buying something.
6 *Thou shalt learn to be a good receiver.* Many of us have trouble receiving graciously and gracefully.

7 ***Thou shalt put music into Christmas.*** Buy several Christmas CD's and play them again and again. Attend church choir cantatas and special Christmas programs. Sing carols with loved ones.

8 ***Thou shalt slow down.*** Remember: Christmas is supposed to be a season of peace, not hypertension.

9 ***Thou shalt remember to worship.*** The church is the place you are most likely to be reminded of the true meaning of Christmas.

10 ***Thou shalt receive Christ into thy life.*** Don't just talk about the Christ of Christmas; receive him into your life as Lord and Savior.

These kinds of reminders can be very beneficial to us as we celebrate the sacred seasons of Advent and Christmas. The truth is that we can get so caught up in the hectic pace of the busyness of Christmas that we miss the message, we miss the meaning, and we can get our priorities terribly mixed up.

The late cartoonist Charles Schulz underscored this truth in one of his classic "Peanuts" comic strips. In the strip, little Sally is lying on a bean bag chair, watching television. Linus is reading to her from a book about the real meaning of Christmas. "Listen to this, Sally," says Linus. "The census which brought Mary and Joseph to Bethlehem is said to have been 'of all the world,' but this probably really means only the Roman Empire of that time. And when we read that there was no room in the inn," Linus continues, "the word *inn* really is better translated as 'guest room.' The intention, of course, is to contrast a place of human lodging with a place for feeding animals. And look at this," Linus says. "The name *Bethlehem* is interesting, too. It literally means 'House of Bread.' I think things like this are so fascinating! What do *you* think, Sally?"

And Sally replies, "I think if I don't get every single thing I want for Christmas this year, I am gonna totally gross out!"

Well, can you relate to this? The question is, How do we keep ourselves from falling into "the Sally trap"? How do we find the true meaning of Christmas? I suspect that we can find it in Bethlehem. Remember what the shepherds said on that first

Christmas night? The angels came and told them about the birth of the Christ Child; and then the shepherds said this: "Let us go over to Bethlehem and see this thing that has happened" (Luke 2:15, RSV).

Let's go with them, you and me! Let's go with the shepherds to Bethlehem. But before we go, we need to be reminded of something that is very important: There is really only one way to go to Bethlehem. You have to go on your knees!

Max Lucado, in his book *The Applause of Heaven*, puts it like this:

> A small cathedral outside Bethlehem marks the supposed birthplace of Jesus. Behind a high altar in the church is a cave, a little cavern lit by silver lamps.
>
> You can enter the main edifice and admire the ancient church. You can also enter the quiet cave where a star embedded in the floor recognizes the birth of the King. There is one stipulation, however. You have to stoop. The door is so low you can't go in standing up.
>
> The same is true of the Christ. You can see the world standing tall, but to witness the Savior, you have to get on your knees.
>
> So . . .
> > while the theologians were sleeping
> > and the elite were dreaming
> > and the successful were snoring,
> > the meek were kneeling.
>
> They were kneeling before the One only the meek will see. They were kneeling in front of Jesus.[1]

So now, in the spirit of humility and in the spirit of expectancy, let us go over to Bethlehem; and let us see this thing that has happened. Let me suggest three things that I am sure we will find there.

First of All, When We Go Over to Bethlehem, We See the Faith That Is Happening There

Some years ago, I was privileged to go with a tour group to the Holy Land. I will never forget that morning when we arrived in Bethlehem. It was such a thrill for me to come to that sacred place where Jesus Christ was born. An older man who was a native of Bethlehem was standing there in front of the church that marks the spot of Jesus' birth. As we walked toward the church, he watched us. Suddenly, the older man waved to me to get my attention; and he said, "Are you an American?"

"Yes," I answered.

"Are you a Christian?"

"Yes!"

He reached over and took my hand in his. He smiled warmly and said, "Welcome! Welcome home!"

That man was right, you know. Bethlehem is the birthplace, the home place, of our faith. It was there that the drama of redemption began. It was there that God came to visit and redeem his people.

There is a fascinating story from some years ago in our country. A young man was caught stealing sheep. He was charged and convicted. The villagers decided to make an example of the young man. They wanted to send a message that sheep stealing would not be tolerated in that small community.

To get their message across dramatically, the villagers did a very harsh thing: They branded his forehead, with the letters "ST," meaning "Sheep Thief." The brand was a constant source of shame to the young man. Penitent, he asked God for forgiveness to help him overcome his problem; and he determined not be be remembered as a thief.

With courage and with God's help, he began to live in a new way. He constantly performed small acts of kindness for everyone. He was kind, thoughtful, helpful, compassionate, and always dependable.

Years and years went by. One day a visitor asked the people of the village what the "ST" on the man's forehead stood for. Strangely, no one could remember. But they told the visitor they suspected that it stood for "Saint"!

Isn't that a wonderful story? That is what "Christmas faith" is all about—how God comes into the world to visit and redeem; how God can turn it around for us; how God can through his grace and love give us a new start, a new beginning, a new chance, a new life.

Christmas reminds us that we are not alone in facing the problems and challenges of the world.

The Olympic Games always produce a number of dramatic and memorable moments. One of the most touching and poignant Olympic moments of all time occurred during the 1992 Summer Olympics in Barcelona, Spain. Perhaps you saw this moment on television or you read about it. It happened during the semifinals of the Men's 400-Meter track race. Great Britain's Derek Redmond went down on the back stretch with a torn right hamstring. Despite the excruciating pain, the injured runner struggled to his feet, fended off medical attendants who had rushed out to help him, and started to hop on one leg in a determined effort to finish the race.

When Redmond reached the stretch, a large man in a T-shirt emerged out of the stands. He pushed his way through the security guards, ran to Derek Redmond, and hugged him. It was Derek Redmond's father. "You don't have to do this," he told his weeping son. "Yes, I do," whispered Derek through his pain. "Well, then," said the father, "we're going to finish this together."

So they did. Waving away the security guards and the medical helpers, the son's head sometimes buried in his father's shoulder, the two men stayed in Derek's lane and crossed the finish line as the crowd gaped, then rose, then cheered, then wept.

This is a great parable for Christmas, isn't it? Realizing that we cannot make it on our own, that we are down and out, that we need help, that we need a Savior, God comes into our world, into our arena, to pick us up, to hold us up, to see us through, and to bring us home. This is the faith of Christmas: "For God so loved the world that he gave his only Son, so that everyone who believes in him may not perish but may have eternal life" (John 3:16).

That is the first thing: Let us go over to Bethlehem and see the faith that is happening there.

Second, When We Go Over to Bethlehem, We See the Hope That Is Happening There

A few years ago, a small Alaskan town called Hope was destroyed by a flood. No lives were lost, but there was tremendous property damage. One of the bishops of the church went there to see how he might help. When he arrived, he found the devastated town completely deserted. However, someone had placed a small sign in the center of what had once been the main street of the little town. The sign read, "The Community of Hope Has Moved to Higher Ground."

This is what the miracle of Christmas does for us. It moves our hope to higher ground. It reminds us of the power and love of God. It reminds us that God is indeed the King of kings, the Prince of Peace, the Lord of heaven and earth, and that God cannot be defeated. Even though evil sometimes will make loud noises in our world, we can be confident and filled with hope because we know that ultimately God and his righteousness will win. And just think of it, God wants to share the victory with us!

That is why the Christ Child came into the world, to bring the good news of God's ultimate victory; and that is our hope.

Some years ago a fire broke out in a hotel in Chicago. Flames and smoke blocked the normal escape routes. Some people on the tenth floor went out onto a balcony to escape the smoke, but they were stuck there. It looked as if they were trapped there and doomed. However, one man in the group braved the smoke and went back into the building. Fortunately, he found an exit to a fire escape. He made his way back through the smoke and flames and told the others he had found a way to safety. Then he led the group out and saved their lives. Another person in the group said later, "You can't imagine the feeling of relief and joy we felt when that man came back for us and said, 'This way out. Follow me. I know the way.' "

This is what the Christian gospel says to us: "Here is One who knows the way to safety and life. Here is One who can deliver you. Here is One who can save you. Follow him and you can live."

At Bethlehem, we find faith, first of all; and second, we find hope.

Third and Finally, When We Go Over to Bethlehem, We Find the Love That Is Happening There

"Love came down at Christmas." That's the way we sing it, and appropriately so, because, most of all, Christmas is about *love*.

My good friend Bill Hinson, in his book *Solid Living in a Shattered World*, tells about a Christmas several years ago when his daughter, Cathy, received a perky, little, white puppy for Christmas. Cathy noticed that the little dog constantly wagged his tail vigorously; so she decided to name him "Happy" because, she said, "He has such a happy ending!"

It became Dad's job to build a doghouse for Happy; but when the new doghouse was completed, Happy wanted no part of it. It was too dark, too big, too foreboding; and the little pup named Happy would not go near the doghouse. When anyone would pick him up and put him in, Happy would run out immediately, trembling and scared to death.

They tried everything: warnings, pleadings, commands, threats, bribes—but to no avail. Nothing worked. Happy the dog would not go into the new doghouse. He was terrified of it.

Finally, Bill said that he gave up in frustration and went into the parsonage to get a drink of water. As he looked out the kitchen window, he could not believe his eyes. He saw Happy with tail joyously wagging trot right into the doghouse and serenely lie down. Bill was amazed; what an incredible change! How could this happen? He went out to investigate.

You know what he found, don't you? His daughter, little Cathy, had crawled into the doghouse and was resting inside. When Happy the dog saw Cathy go inside, he trotted right in there beside her and made it his home. The point is clear: Where all those other things had failed, love prevailed. That is what Christmas teaches us: Love is the single most powerful thing in the world.

The shepherds said, "Let us go over to Bethlehem and see

this thing that has happened" (Luke 2:15, RSV). When we go to Bethlehem, there are three things we will see there clearly (I am sure of it!):

> the miracle of faith
> the miracle of hope
> the miracle of love!

Study / Discussion Questions

1. Reread Luke 2:15-20. Why do you think the angels appeared to the shepherds and not to others in the area? What was the shepherds' reaction after seeing the baby Jesus? How do you think their lives were changed?
2. If you had to select just one, which of the "Ten Commandments for Christmas" would be first in importance for you this year? Why? What causes us to get our priorities so mixed up at times?
3. Why should a journey of faith begin at Bethlehem? What expectations should we have as we begin our faith journey? What expectations should we have for the season of Advent?
4. In what ways would you like your faith to grow during Advent? What activities stimulate faith?
5. Name some of the secular and non-secular hopes we have as Christmas approaches. What does God remind us about hope when Christmas arrives? How does our journey of hope continue after Christmas?

Prayer

God, we thank you for the many gifts you give us during the season of Advent. Strengthen our faith so that we may see your love and presence more clearly as Christmas approaches. Amen.

Focus for the Week

Think about your faith this week. How has it been challenged? How has it been strengthened? What activity or person has influenced it the most? How has your faith influenced others?

NOTE

[1] From *The Applause of Heaven*, by Max Lucado (Copyright © 1990 by Max Lucado); page 73.

Let Us Go Over to Bethlehem and Find the Promise of Christmas

Scripture: Read Matthew 1:16-25.

The noted British poet and theologian G.K. Chesterton was a brilliant man who could think deep thoughts and express them well. However, he was also extremely absent-minded; and over the years he became rather notorious for getting lost. He would just absolutely forget where he was supposed to be and what he was supposed to be doing.

On one such occasion, he sent a telegram to his wife with these words: "Seems that I'm lost again. Presently, I am at Market Harborough. Where ought I to be?" As only a spouse could say it, she telegraphed back a one-word reply: "Home!"

That is precisely what this classic passage in the first chapter of Matthew does for us. It brings us home to the real meaning of Christmas, home to the most magnificent truth in all of the Bible, home to our Lord's greatest promise, namely this: "God is with us"! When we accept Jesus Christ into our lives, nothing, not even death, can separate us from God and his love. "God is with us." That is what Christmas is about. "God is with us"; the great people of faith have always claimed that promise.

Just think of it: Moses, caught between the pharaoh and the sea in a seemingly hopeless situation, believed that God was with him. Moses went forward and trusted God to open a way, and God did! Shadrach, Meshach, and Abednego went into the fiery furnace, into a seemingly hopeless situation; and they trusted God to be with them, and God was! Little David stood before Goliath. What chance could a small boy with a slingshot have against this giant of a warrior? But David believed that God was with him, and this made all the difference!

Now, it is interesting to note that when the writer of Matthew's Gospel wanted to capture the meaning of Christmas, the meaning of the Christ event, the meaning of Jesus, in a single word, he did a very wise thing. The Gospel writer reached back into the Old Testament, pulled out an old word, dusted it off, and used it to convey the message. The word was *Emmanuel* (see Isaiah 7:14). That is what Jesus is about. "They shall name him Emmanuel," which, as we have already noted, means "God is with us."

The impact of this promise is incredible. When you believe that "God is with us," when you accept that, when you claim that promise, it will absolutely change your life! Let me show you what I mean by bringing this closer to home. Let me underscore three ideas that are related to this great promise of God's presence with us. I am sure that you will think of other examples; but for now, please consider these.

"God Is With Us": We Can Claim That Promise, First of All, When We Are Frightened

All of us get frightened or scared sometimes. Jesus sensed this, and consequently he talked about it quite a lot. The words *fear, anxious, troubled, fretful,* and *afraid* were often in his speech. "Fear not"; "fret no more"; "don't be anxious"; "let not your hearts be troubled"; "don't be afraid." Jesus spoke words like these often because he saw lots of fears and anxieties in the lives of those he loved.

It is still true today. Everywhere we look, we see people doing battle with their fears. There is the little child who is afraid of the dark, afraid of being separated from her parents, afraid to go to school. Or the young person who wants to step out on his own and take on the world but is afraid. There is the mother afraid for her children, the executive afraid that this year's profits may not be as good as projected, or the factory worker afraid that a massive lay-off is on the way.

In one way or another, fear threatens us all.

But then along comes Christmas with the great promise that calms our fears: Emmanuel, "God is with us."

Storm clouds and strong gusts of wind came up suddenly over the elementary school in the midwest. The school's public address system blared tornado warnings. It was too dangerous to send the children home. Instead, they were taken to the basement, where the children lined the walls and huddled together in fear. The teachers were worried too.

To help ease the tension, the principal suggested a sing-along. But the voices were weak and unenthusiastic. One child after another began to cry. The children could not be consoled and were close to panic. Then, one of the teachers, whose faith seemed equal to any emergency, whispered to the child closest to her, "Janie, I know you are scared. I am too, but aren't we forgetting something? There is a power greater than any storm. God will protect us. Just say to yourself, 'God is with us,' then pass the words on to the child next to you, and tell her to pass it on."

Suddenly, that dark and cold basement became a sacred place, as each child in turn whispered around the room those powerful words, "God is with us." "God is with us." "God is with us."

A sense of peace and courage and confidence settled over the group. One of the teachers said, "I could hear the wind outside still blowing with such strength that it literally shook the building, but it did not seem to matter now. Inside, the fears subsided; and tears faded away. When the all-clear signal came some time later, students and staff returned to the classrooms without the usual jostling and talking. Through the years I have remembered those calming words. In times of stress and trouble, I have been able again and again to find release from fear or tension by repeating those calming words: 'God is with us!' 'God is with us!'"

Emmanuel, "God is with us." We can claim that great promise, first of all, when we are frightened. We can claim that great promise. That is number one.

Second, We Can Claim That Promise When We Are Lonely

There are lots of lonely people in the world who desperately need to hear the good news of Christmas.

The great Old Testament scholar Martin Buber said something toward the end of his life that touched me greatly. It is something we all would do well to remember.

Buber was commenting on that wonderful scene in the book of Exodus where God appears to Moses in the burning bush. Moses asks God, "What is your name?" God answers, "I AM WHO I AM."

After studying the original Hebrew text for many years, Buber said he had come to the conclusion that we have mistranslated that verse. He indicated that instead of translating the name of God as "I AM WHO I AM," it should read, "I Shall Be There"!

Isn't that beautiful? The name of God is "I Shall Be There"! This is the greatest promise in all of the Bible, God's promise to always be there for us.

Think of it like this: When we have to face the pharaohs of life, the name of God is "I Shall Be There"! When we are scared or hurting or sad, the name of God is "I Shall Be There"! When we have to face sickness or heartache or even death, the name of God is "I Shall Be There"!

Christmas reminds us dramatically and powerfully that our God is a "seeking, saving God" who wants passionately to come to us and bring us into the circle of his love. So, it helps to remember that when we are frightened and when we are lonely, we can always claim the promise of God's presence with us because the name of God is "Emmanuel"; the name of God is "I Shall Be There"!

Third and Finally, We Can Claim That Promise When We Are in Sorrow

It seems like it would be easy to feel the presence of God when we are on top of the world and all the breaks are going our way; but actually the reverse is true: God is never nearer to us than when we are hurting. There are two reasons for this.

First, I think we are more open to God when we are in need. Second, I believe God is like a loving parent who wants especially to be with his children when they are in pain.

Recently, I was with some friends who were experiencing a very difficult and grievous situation; they said, "This is so hard to take. Our hearts are broken, but we're going to make it because God is with us as never before. He is with us, giving us his strength."

More recently, another good friend placed on my desk a poignant prayer-poem and suggested that it might be helpful to all those in our church who make hospital visits. It is called "Prayers in a Hospital Elevator," and it says it all. This prayer-poem has two verses. The first verse is entitled "Going Up," and it reads like this:

What am I going to say to him, Lord?
He's dying,
But the family
doesn't want
him to know.
They're having trouble facing it.
Shall I be cheerful? Or solemn?
Either way
I'd be self-conscious
And that's no good.
Do I play games
Pretend that he'll get well?
What would you do, Lord?
Maybe I should pray with him
After all
he's a Christian, Lord.

But would praying together
make him think
that I thought
he was dying?
I wish I knew
what to do, Lord
Excuse me; this is my floor.

The second verse is entitled "Going Down":

Well, Lord, that was a surprise.
I hardly said a word.
It was he
who did the talking.
The smile on his pale face
almost broke me up.
He seemed so glad to see me
and he held my hand so tight.
How concerned he was
about his family.
At a time like that!
It made me feel pretty small.
When he said he knew the situation,
that he knew he wouldn't leave
that room alive . . .
I actually felt relieved that he knew.
When he said he wasn't afraid
had no regrets
I could have cried.
And when we prayed together
I was convinced . . .
as he already was
that death is nothing to be feared.
So why was I worried about visiting him?
Didn't I know all along
That You would be there, Lord?
(Written by Robert J. McMullen, Jr., Charlotte, NC. Reprinted with permission.)

This is the good news of Christmas, isn't it? This is the good news of the Christian faith. Emmanuel. God is with us. When we are frightened, when we are lonely, when we are in sorrow and at lots of other times, we can claim that promise! *God is with us.*

Study / Discussion Questions

1. Recall a difficult time in your life when the promise "God is with us" helped you or your family to overcome a challenge. How was the presence of God made known? How did you feel when you claimed God's promise?
2. How has your faith in God helped you to claim victory over fear? What fears do some persons have during this season of the year? How can you help others with their fears?
3. What can cause people to be lonely as Christmas approaches? Describe a lonely Christmas you have had, or explain why you believe you have not experienced a lonely Christmas. How can you help persons who are lonely? How have others helped you in times when you felt alone?
4. How does sorrow bring us closer to God and to one another? What are some things that can trigger sorrow? How can the promises of God help you fight sorrow? Recall a time when you experienced sorrow and how you dealt with it.
5. How has the promise "God is with us" changed your life? Why did God give us this promise? Name some ways in which we can share this promise with others during Advent.

Prayer

God, you are always with us. Your promises deliver us from the cares of this world. Thank you for your love and for the gifts you so freely give to us each day. May we share your love with others. Amen.

Focus for the Week

This week, focus on the promises of God. Begin by using your Bible to locate God's promises to you. Write down some of these promises, and carry them with you during the week. Reflect on them often, and look for opportunities to share God's promises with others.

Let Us Go Over to Bethlehem and Find the Peace of Christmas

Scripture: Read Isaiah 9:6-7; 51:7-10; Luke 2:13-14.

It was a dark night in the year 1741. A musician named George Frederick Handel stumbled blindly down a dark street in London. Handel had fallen on hard times. He was depressed, despondent, filled with despair. Jealous rivalries, ill health, and a series of devastating misfortunes had brought him to this low ebb. He felt empty, dejected, lonely, hopeless, and miserable.

A cerebral hemorrhage had caused a partial paralysis in Handel. His eyes were beginning to fail him. His creativity had all but disappeared in the cloud of troubles that enveloped his life. His self-esteem was shot, and he was haunted by self-doubts. He was unhappy with himself, at odds with his friends; and he had drifted away from God. Nearing the age of sixty, his income gone and his health shattered, Handel felt certain that his life was over.

In this defeated frame of mind, he returned that dismal night to his shabby home. When he arrived there, he found a large package at his door. He literally clawed open the seal. In the package he found the words to a new sacred piece of music and a letter from Charles Jennens, asking Handel to write the music for it.

Still in despair, George Frederick Handel began to leaf carelessly through the pages. Suddenly his eyes fell upon a passage that captivated him. It read, "He was despised and rejected. He looked for someone to have pity on him, but there was no one—neither found he anyone to comfort him." Handel resonated to those words. Those words, written originally about Jesus, actually described what Handel himself was feeling at that moment—despised, rejected, and alone.

With a growing sense of kinship, Handel read on; and he found these words: "He trusted in God and God did not leave (him)...God gave him rest." Now the words began to come alive and to glow with meaning for Handel! They stirred his soul and warmed his heart. He read on: "I know that my redeemer liveth. Rejoice. Rejoice. Hallelujah!"

George Frederick Handel could feel the creative forces resurrecting and surging within him once again. Wondrous, incredible melodies straight from heaven rapidly tumbled, one after another, into his mind. He grabbed pen and paper and began to fill page after page with amazing confidence and swiftness. All through the night, he wrote. Breakfast was brought in to him the next day, but he would not stop to eat.

Day after day, the old master worked vigorously, ignoring all who came into the room. He was riveted to his work. Sometimes he became so moved by what he was writing that he wept and shouted. At last, he finished. Exhausted, he fell onto his bed and slept peacefully for seventeen hours. But on his desk was the musical score of one of the greatest and most beloved pieces of sacred music ever written: Handel's *Messiah*!

In later years, Handel was beset by many more infirmities; but he never gave in to despair again. He became blind, but his spirit remained undaunted to the end; for in his heart was the music of *Messiah*, along with the sure knowledge that God held the key to life.

Now, what had happened to George Frederick Handel? What had made that dramatic change? What had turned it around for him? Simply this: He experienced Christmas! He received the Messiah! Christ was born afresh in the manger of Handel's heart, and it made him a new person.

Have you heard about the young woman who lived on a large ranch in West Texas? She had fallen in love with a local cowboy named Tex, and she wanted to get married. But Tex was inexperienced in the world of romance; and to make matters worse, he was extremely shy. The woman realized that she needed to help him a bit in order to move this courtship along.

"Oh, Tex," she said, "do you think my eyes are like the glittering stars?"

"Yep," he replied.

"And do you think my teeth are like a beautiful string of pearls?" she asked.

"Yep," Tex answered.

"And do you think my complexion is like gorgeous rose petals?" she questioned.

"Yep," he replied.

"And do you think my hair shines like gold in the moonlight?"

"Yep," he answered.

"Oh, Tex!" she exclaimed. "You say the most wonderful things."

Well, let me tell you something: Christmas has some wonderful things to say to us. Christmas has some wonderful things to do for us. Christmas has some wonderful things to give to us. But we have to have the ears of faith to hear them, the eyes of faith to see them, the heart of faith to feel them, and the grace of God to accept them.

One of the best gifts Christmas gives us is the gift of peace. This is one of the key themes, isn't it? "Peace on earth, goodwill toward all." Christ is the Prince of Peace. He brings the peace that passes all understanding. He comes to visit and redeem his people and to guide our feet into the way of peace. That is the way the Bible puts it.

This is precisely what happened to George Frederick Handel. Christ brought peace to his anguished spirit. Handel was frustrated with himself, cut off from other people, at odds with God; but then Christ was born anew in his heart. Christ stilled the storms in his life that were tearing him apart, and he became a new person. And where there had been strife, now there was peace. Where there had been fear, now there was courage. And where there had been emptiness, now there was incredible creativity.

That is the way it works. Christmas is the dramatic reminder that Christ came into this world to redeem us and to bring peace to our troubled souls. If in faith we will accept it, Christmas has a great gift for us: the gift of *peace*. Christmas offers us peace within, peace with others, and peace with God; but we have to accept the gift. Let's take a look at these three ideas.

First of All, Christmas Gives Us Peace Within

In the movie *Home Alone*, a little boy named Kevin is accidentally left behind when his family leaves for a European vacation. On Christmas Eve, Kevin begins to feel sad and lonely; so he goes to church. There he meets an older man who is also unhappy because of family problems. As they engage in conversation, young Kevin admits that he feels guilty because he knows that he did not always treat his family right, but now he misses them terribly. "Well," says the older man, "you're in church now, and this is the place to come when you're feeling bad about yourself."

He was right, wasn't he? The church, which exists *because* of Christmas, is *indeed* the place to come when we need comfort, when we need forgiveness, when we need to make a new start, when we need peace for our troubled souls. The Christ of Christmas is our personal Savior because there is a hole in our souls that only he can fill. Remember how Augustine put it: "Our souls are restless, O Lord, until they find their rest in Thee."

One day very close to Christmas, a young boy was coming down the hallway at church. He had in his hand a little ceramic tray that he had made in Sunday school. It was to be his Christmas gift to his mother. He had been working on it for several weeks, and he was so proud of it.

As he ran down the hall, he tripped and fell. The tray crashed to the floor and broke into several pieces. The little boy was devastated. He began to cry loudly and uncontrollably. He was absolutely heartbroken.

People tried to comfort him with all kinds of counsel: "It was just a tray. Not worth much. No big loss. Besides, you can make another one. It's nothing. Forget it. You can give your mother something else. Don't worry about it." But nothing helped. The child was inconsolable.

Finally, his mother arrived on the scene. Quickly, she realized what had happened. Kneeling down beside her crestfallen, distraught son, with his broken gift, she hugged him tightly and said, "Well, now, I think this is fixable. Let's pick up the pieces and take it all home. We'll put it back together and see what we can make of it!" The little boy hugged his mother back and smiled.

Isn't that exactly what the Christmas message is about? The world is broken into many fragments, as are our lives. And God stoops down beside us. He hugs us and says, "Well, now, this is fixable. Let me help you pick up the pieces. We'll put it back together and see what we can make of it!"

First of all, Christmas offers us the gift of inner peace, peace within; but we have to *accept* that gift.

Second, Christmas Gives Us Peace With Others

Isn't it sad, when you stop to think about it, how out-of-sorts people can get with one another, how estranged people can become, how hostile they can feel toward one another? When will we ever learn? We spend weary days and sleepless nights brooding over our resentments, calculating ways to get even. We demand our "pound of flesh," seethe over our grievances, and wallow in our self-pity, shackled by our silly pride, unbending, unmerciful, unable and unwilling to forgive and reconcile. Isn't that tragic?

A cruel word is finally only an echo. Revenge actually is never sweet; it ultimately becomes a sour stomach and a bitter memory. Violence only breeds more violence. Hate poisons the soul. Resentment, jealousy, bigotry, prejudice—these are spiritual viruses that will absolutely make us sick! Jesus knew this; and he came into this world to show us how to be peacemakers, bridge-builders, and reconcilers, to show us how to seek forgiveness and to offer it. That is why we call him the Prince of Peace.

Some years ago, hall-of-fame baseball player Hank Aaron was checking into a hotel up east. The young desk clerk told him that they were full up, and there were no rooms available. However, the hotel manager recognized the baseball superstar. He rushed over to the desk clerk and said, "Don't you know who this is? This is the great Hank Aaron of the Atlanta Braves. He just broke Babe Ruth's homerun record."

"Oh I'm terribly sorry, Mr. Aaron," said the desk clerk. "Of course we can find a room for you." And then the clerk said, "Why didn't you tell me you were somebody?"

I love Hank Aaron's response. He said, "Son, everybody is somebody!"

That is what Christmas tells us: Everybody is somebody! But more, everybody is somebody for whom Christ came and for whom Christ died.

If we could always remember that and treat everybody we meet with that kind of love and respect, what a difference that would make in our relationships! What a difference that would make in our world! Listen! If you are estranged from anybody, at odds with anyone, do not let that hostility go on! Go fix it today. Go set it right. With the help of God, go make peace today.

Christmas offers us the gift of peace within and the gift of peace with others; but we have to *accept* those gifts.

Third and Finally, Christmas Gives Us Peace With God

It was two days before Christmas. There was a long line at the post office as people were frantically trying to use overnight mail to get Christmas packages to others on time. A woman with three little girls in tow finally reached the counter. "Can you get this package to Phoenix, Arizona, tomorrow?" she asked.

"I can, lady; but it will cost you."

"How much?"

"Forty-seven dollars and forty cents."

"Gracious!" she said. "That's a lot, but I've got to do it. This present is for my father. It has to be there before Christmas because, you see, Christmas is also his birthday."

"Man! What a bum deal *that* is!" said the postal clerk. "I sure am glad I don't know anyone born on Christmas!"

Someone in the line spoke up: "I sure am glad I do!"

Let me ask you something. Do you know the one born on Christmas day? *Do* you? Do you really know him as Lord and Savior? Do you know this one who came to visit and redeem and save? Have you accepted him into you life? Has he been born in your heart? The hymn writer put it like this:

> Hark! the herald angels sing,
> "Glory to the new-born King;
> Peace on earth, and mercy mild,
> God and sinners reconciled!"
> Joyful, all ye nations rise,
> Join the triumph of the skies;
> With th'angelic host proclaim,
> Christ is born in Bethlehem!

> Born that we no more may die,
> Born to raise us from the earth,
> Born to give us second birth.[1]

Jesus Christ, our Lord and Savior, was born to give us peace within, peace with others, and peace with God.

Study / Discussion Questions

1. In your own words, explain what peace means to you. What gives you peace? Does peace come with a cost? Explain your answers.
2. Share a time that you were given the gift of peace during Advent or Christmas. Who gave you this gift? How did you feel? How were you changed because of it?

3. What impressed you about the story of Handel? How did he gain peace within? What is needed to accept the gift of peace?

4. Why is it sometimes more difficult to be at peace with others during Advent and Christmas? Why is it important to be at peace with others? How can we share the peace of God with one another this season?

5. What do you think it means to be at peace with God? Does peace come from God's actions or from our actions, or does it come from both? In what way is peace God's Christmas gift to you?

Prayer

Jesus, you are the Prince of Peace. Our world and our troubled lives yearn for peace. May we remember that you are the source of peace, that it is your gift, and that it is always available to us. Amen.

Focus for the Week

Meditate on peace during the coming week. Consider the ways in which you would like to experience God's peace during this season of Advent. Look for opportunities to be an instrument of God's peace in your daily routine.

NOTE

[1] From "Hark! the Herald Angels Sing," by Charles Wesley, in *The United Methodist Hymnal* (Copyright © 1989 The United Methodist Publishing House); 240.

Let Us Go Over to Bethlehem and Find the Christ of Christmas

Scripture: Read Luke 2:1-21.

Are you familiar with the name Tom Bodett? If you do not recognize the name, you would recognize the voice. He is the guy who does those homespun Motel 6 commercials that always end with these words: "Drop on by; we'll leave the light on for you."

Tom Bodett, in his "down-home" way, recently announced that he has started a new club. He calls it the G.N.T. club. The G.N.T. stands for the **G**roup that **N**otices **T**hings. Tom says that one charter member of the G.N.T. club is a young woman he met in the grocery store.

Tom was behind her in the checkout line. She had a basket full of groceries. He had a package of chewing gum. She noticed and said, "You only have one item. Please go ahead of me." And that, Tom Bodett says, made her eligible for entrance into the G.N.T. club, the Group that Notices Things and then does something about it.

Tom Bodett also tells about a man he saw on a busy Alaska highway. Tom reported that he came over a hill and saw this man standing out on the road, waving to slow people down, and then directing them around this treacherous spot of ice on the highway. This man was not an official, not a police officer, not a highway patrolman. He was just an ordinary citizen who saw a potentially dangerous situation, pulled his truck over to the side of the road, and got out and did something about it. And that, Tom Bodett says, qualifies him for membership in the G.N.T. club.

He goes on to mention others, like a young girl who sees a banana peel on the sidewalk, picks it up, and throws it into the trash; an older couple holding hands and watching a beautiful sunset; a group of teenage boys working together to rescue a frightened cat from a tall tree; a mission team from a local church who just show up one day to refurbish the home of a lady in her nineties. All these folks Tom Bodett calls charter members of the G.N.T. club, the Group that Notices Things and then does something about it.

When I heard about the G.N.T. club, interestingly, I thought immediately of the shepherds in the Christmas story. That is what *they* did. They noticed things and acted. They noticed things and responded. They noticed things and did something about it. Let me show you what I mean.

First of All, the Shepherds Saw the Angel

They took notice of the angel of Christmas.

Now, I know what you are probably thinking: *Well, of course they saw the angel! How could they miss that? The angel appeared dramatically. The glory of the Lord shone around them brightly. The angel told them boldly about the baby in the manger in Bethlehem. And then the angelic chorus broke into song: "Glory to God in the highest . . ." You couldn't miss that, could you?* And yet as powerful as that was, as glorious as that was, and as dramatic as that was, *no one else noticed.* According to the Bible, Bethlehem and the surrounding regions were jampacked with people that night. But only the shepherds saw the angel; only the shepherds took notice.

Angels are messengers from God. Only those with the eyes of faith can see them; only those with the ears of faith can hear them: and only those with hearts of faith can sense and feel their presence.

A few years ago, the *Houston Chronicle* did a nice thing. They printed a series of holiday stories submitted by readers. One story appeared in the paper each day. One of the stories came

41

from Cynthia Thomas, a chaplain at St. Luke's Hospital. Read her words:

It was my first Christmas back in Houston, and I was dreading the season. With friends and family far away, I felt lonely and unloved. Even God, it seemed, had abandoned me.

I did not expect my best Christmas gift to be a woman dressed like a package. I had dropped by the M.D. Anderson chapel to watch some fellow employees tape their Christmas musical.

It was there that I encountered a small, frail, middle-aged patient. She was totally "wrapped." A turban covered her bald head, the signature side effect of chemotherapy. A face mask protected her from germs. Her wheelchair was draped with sheets and blankets.

As the choir performed, the patient sat nearby singing Handel's "Messiah" with all her heart. Probably only her husband and God could hear her, but her spirit was soaring all over the room.

While everything about her physical body whispered sickness and death, a love that transcends death poured from that frame. She sang with abandon, her pale, thin face luminous and eyes glittering.

In the middle of this struggle of her life, this woman was praising God. And in her joyful expression, it was as if Jesus were saying to me, "I don't leave when times are hard. Just as I love this woman, I love you."

If I ran into this patient today, I would have no idea who she is, but for a moment she became God's instrument for me.

I have a Christmas memory—of seeing God through a patient—and I remember her as a very special gift.[1]

Cynthia Thomas, the chaplain who wrote this touching holiday story, had seen the angel of Christmas in a most unlikely place. She had seen the angel of Christmas in a hospital patient.

Listen! The angels of Christmas are all around us. Messengers from God are all around us. The question is, Do we have the eyes of faith to see them, the ears of faith to hear them, and the hearts of faith to sense and feel their presence?

First of all, the shepherds belong in the G.N.T. club because they saw the angel.

Second, They Saw the Christ Child

A minister once told a true and poignant story about being invited to a party one day to celebrate a wedding. He arrived late. He really did not know anyone there except the friend who had invited him. Everyone seemed in high spirits, dancing, laughing, singing, eating, and visiting. Apparently everyone was having a good time.

As the evening progressed, however, the minister said that he noticed a beautiful young woman sitting at a table all by herself. No one was paying any attention to her at all. When the minister asked his friend who she was, his friend replied, "Don't you know? I must introduce you to her. She is the bride!" The minister concluded by saying, "Can you imagine that? Can you imagine being left alone and unnoticed at your own wedding party? Can you imagine being ignored on your 'big day'?"

Is this perhaps how Jesus must sometimes feel at Christmas? Some people come to the Christmas party and ignore the guest of honor.

The shepherds did not make that mistake. They had their priorities straight. They dropped everything and rushed to the manger to see the newborn King of kings. The shepherds belong in the G.N.T club because they saw the angel and they saw the Christ Child.

Third and Finally, They Saw the Good News of Christmas

About this time each year they show it on television: Dr. Seuss' classic story, *How the Grinch Stole Christmas*. You are probably familiar with it. The Grinch was a sinister character who despised the celebration of Christmas. The people of Whoville loved Christmas, and their celebration of Christmas irritated the grouchy Grinch. The people of Whoville would gather on Christmas Day around their beautifully decorated trees. The people would sing and laugh and play with great happiness as they opened their presents, tasted the sweets from their Christmas stockings, and celebrated the great joy of the day. Oh, how the Grinch hated the sound of it all!

So the Grinch hatched an evil plan. He would show them. He would steal their Christmas. This would stop all their laughing and singing and Christmas noise!

The Grinch disguised himself as Santa Claus; and he went from house to house, stealing all the toys and presents and sweets of Christmas. He was so proud of himself and his evil deed! On Christmas morning, he waited with baited breath to hear the sounds of sadness when the people of Whoville discovered that their Christmas had been stolen. But to his amazement, what he heard was not the sound of crying and moaning. What he heard was the same sound of joy he had always heard. The people of Whoville were singing and laughing and celebrating as always the joy of Christmas Day!

The point is clear: If the Christ Child is born in your heart, no one can steal your Christmas! For you see, the real joy of Christmas is not in material presents (nice as they are); no, it is in receiving the only gift of Christmas that really matters, the gift of God's love in Jesus Christ, the Gift that was wrapped in heaven. The shepherds saw it. Remember how the Scriptures put it: "The shepherds returned, glorifying and praising God for all they had heard and seen" (Luke 2:20). They were charter members of the G.N.T. club, for they saw the angel, they saw the Christ Child, and they saw the good news of Christmas.

Christmas invites us to break out of the Frequent-flyer Syndrome and join the G.N.T. club, the Group that Notices Things, so that we can see and embrace the faith of Christmas; the promise of Christmas; the peace of Christ; and, most important, the Christ of Christmas.

Study / Discussion Questions

1. Share a time when you noticed a person in need, responded, and made a difference. How did you feel? What made you notice? What motivated you to respond?
2. Recall a time when you were ministered to at Christmas by

an angel, or reflect upon and share about a situation where you witnessed an angel in action. How did you know the person was an angel?

3. What causes people to miss seeing the Christ Child at Christmas? In what ways can we open our own eyes and the eyes of others to see the Christ Child at Christmas?

4. What does it mean to see the good news of Christmas? How does the good news change us and others? How can we share the good news during Advent?

5. What person or activity has made the Christmas story come alive for you? Share how your faith has grown over the years. For you, what makes Christmas start to become less about presents and more about the birth of Jesus Christ?

Prayer

God, thank you for the gift of Jesus. Help us to remember that Jesus is the meaning of Christmas. Slow us down, Lord, so that we may see the real gifts you offer to us each and every day. Amen.

Focus for the Week

Reflect each day of the coming week on what it means to be a recipient of the gift of God's love in Jesus Christ. Think about how you should live your life because you have been given this fantastic gift from God. How has this gift changed your life? How do you want your life to change in the future because of this gift?

NOTE

[1] From "Patient Reveals the Spirit of Holiday," by Cynthia Thomas, in the *Houston Chronicle*, Dec. 4, 1995.